System Administrator Learning PowerShell

A Book for Inspiring IT Professionals who want to Expand their Skills in PowerShell. Become a valuable IT Member.

NAKA MOTO

NAKA MOTO

Table of Contents

NAKA MOTO

Top PowerShell Commands

PowerShell accepts syntax from Linux and Command Prompt. Certain commands are also compatible with PowerShell from these languages. To become more familiarized with the syntax of PowerShell here are the top commands. Notice the structure of the commands.

Navigating the File System

Get-ChildItem: Lists items in a directory.

Set-Location: Changes the current directory.

Push-Location: Saves the current directory on a stack so you can return to it.

Pop-Location: Returns to the directory saved by Push-Location.

File Manipulation

New-Item: Creates a new file or directory.

Remove-Item: Deletes a file or directory.

Copy-Item: Copies a file or directory to another location.

Move-Item: Moves a file or directory to a new location.

Rename-Item: Renames a file or directory.

System Administration

Get-Service: Lists all services on a computer.

Start-Service: Starts a stopped service.

Stop-Service: Stops a running service.

Restart-Service: Restarts a service.

User & Permissions Management

Get-LocalUser: Retrieves local user accounts.

New-LocalUser: Creates a new local user account.

Remove-LocalUser: Deletes a local user account.

Get-Acl: Gets access control list (ACL) for a file or resource.

Set-Acl: Sets the ACL for a file or resource.

Networking Commands

Test-Connection: Sends ICMP echo requests to a target host to test connectivity.

Get-NetIPAddress: Retrieves IP address configuration.

Get-NetAdapter: Lists network adapters.

Resolve-DnsName: Resolves a DNS name to an IP address.

Process Management

Get-Process: Lists currently running processes.

Start-Process: Starts a new process.

Stop-Process: Stops a running process.

Wait-Process: Waits for a process to exit.

Working With Objects

Select-Object: Selects specific properties of an object.

Where-Object: Filters objects based on property values.

Sort-Object: Sorts objects by property values.

Group-Object: Groups objects by property values.

Finding Files | *Removing Files*

As a Sys Admin you will be tasked with finding specific files and then removing them or replacing them. Here are the basic scripts. Our example will include some real-life applications.

1. **Find files by name**:
Get-ChildItem -Path "C:\Path\To\Directory" -Filter "filename.ext" -Recurse

This command searches for files named filename.ext in the specified directory and all its subdirectories.

2. **Find files by extension**:
Get-ChildItem -Path "C:\Path\To\Directory" -Filter "*.ext" -Recurse

This command searches for all files with the .ext extension in the specified directory and its subdirectories.

3. **Find files by date modified**:
Get-ChildItem -Path "C:\Path\To\Directory" -Recurse | Where-Object { $_.LastWriteTime -gt (Get-Date).AddDays(-7) }

This command finds all files modified in the last 7 days.

4. **Find files by size**:
Get-ChildItem -Path "C:\Path\To\Directory" -Recurse | Where-Object { $_.Length -gt 1MB }

This command finds all files larger than 1MB.

5. **Find files by content**:
Get-ChildItem -Path "C:\Path\To\Directory" -Recurse | Select-String -Pattern "search text"

SYSTEM ADMINISTRATOR LEARNING POWERSHELL

*Represents a wildcard * will recurse through all users in filepath.*
Most Shortcuts are a .lnk file

Finding Shortcuts on Desktop
Get-ChildItem -Path "C:\Users*\Desktop" -Filter "filename.lnk" -Recurse

Finding .pst files
Get-ChildItem -force -Path "C:\Users*\AppData\Local\Microsoft\Outlook " -Filter "*.pst" -Recurse

Automation

One-liners are great to improve efficiency and have better code clarity! Now we want to encapsulate our payload within a structure that can traverse the network, exciting stuff! There are many ways to do this but for the sake of consistency throughout our lessons we will be using a method that minimizes messiness. Try to understand this code before I reveal the answer. Can you find where our payload will go?

```
### Enter computer names as a new line in .txt file###
$complist = Get-Content "C:\computerList.txt"
## Iterate thru list##
foreach ($comp in $complist){
        ##Test Connection to machine##
$pingtest = Test-Connection -ComputerName $comp -Quiet -Count 1 -ErrorAction SilentlyContinue
        ##If machine pings search for file##
                if($pingtest){  }}
```

Answer

```
### Enter computer names as a new line in .txt file###
$complist = Get-Content "C:\computerList.txt"
## Iterate thru list##
foreach ($comp in $complist){
        ##Test Connection to machine##
$pingtest = Test-Connection -ComputerName $comp -Quiet -Count 1 -ErrorAction SilentlyContinue
        ##If machine pings search for file##
                if($pingtest){
Invoke-Command -computername $comp -scriptblock{Get-ChildItem -force -Path
"C:\Users\*\AppData\Local\Microsoft\Outlook" -Filter "*.pst" -Recurse}
                }}
```

To summarize, we have our targets in a .txt file separated with a new line like this,

Host1

Host2

Host3

We are testing if the host is online and then outputting all file paths with hits to a new file locally. The path used in our script is the default path for Outlook .pst files. The user may have the .pst file in another location. Also note, *AppData* is a hidden folder. To traverse this branch, you must use the parameter **-Force**

Removal

To remove the file, add | Remove-Item to the end of the payload.

Invoke-Command -computername $comp -scriptblock{Get-ChildItem -force -Path "C:\Users*\AppData\Local\Microsoft\Outlook" -Filter "*.pst" -Recurse} | Remove-Item

Summary

Finding files or folders within a machine is a very useful tool for an administrator. This command is also a very difficult one to put together. It is rather long, bulky, and will need to be adjusted for your specific search. Keep these scripts available for the moment you need to use such a tool.

As your knowledge of Windows Systems grow you will learn where apps store file paths that that are commonly used for troubleshooting by system administrators. This file path is where Outlook OST and PST files are stored.

We will develop this command in a future chapter to perform a registry query.

Installing | *Uninstalling*

System Administrators are turned to for installation/uninstallation of programs. Admins must perform installs and uninstalls. Clicking install and uninstall is such a trivial task especially with the use of a GUI. As a System Administrator we need to bend the computer to our will and show a greater grasp of the internal concepts. This will help us expand our knowledge base and visualize deeper concepts.

I want to showcase in this chapter how to perform installations and uninstallations through PowerShell without the granting of administrator rights to the user.

When performing the task remotely we need to capture a baseline for installed programs.

To capture installed programs on a machine :

Wmic product list

Uninstallation

To perform the uninstall we must grab the GUID of the program. The GUID can be found in different places but let's head to the registry to get the GUID.

HKEY_LOCAL_MACHINE\SOFTWARE\Microsoft\Windows\CurrentVersion\Uninstall\

Traverse the registry keys until you find the program. The entry contains the GUID. Now we can perform the uninstall.

start-process -FilePath "msiexec.exe" -ArgumentList "/x {GUID} /QN /NORESTART" -wait

Summary: Here we are calling msiexec.exe process using a -filepath switch to indicate the exact location. You can adjust the path for your target system. Argument List switch contains /x=uninstall the GUID program, /QN is silent uninstall, /NORESTART keeps the PC on, and -wait waits for completion. Quote the entire Argument list as these switches are passed as a string to the command

Another option for uninstalling programs is to use the uninstall-Package cmdlet. This option requires Finding the name of the program to be uninstalled.

Control Panel > Programs & Features > Name

To find the program name using PowerShell:
Get-Package "Name of Program*"

To remove the program using Uninstall-Package cmdlet:
Uninstall-package 'program name'

This looks like:

Get-Package "Name of Program*" | Uninstall-Package

This works out well if you have different versions of a program. We include a wild card at the end of the name to retrieve any version of this program.

Automation

The next question for a System Administrator is always how can we automate this process? Now that we have a shell for automation from our last chapter, we can insert the new payload into our automation shell.

```
### Enter computer names as a new line in .txt file###
$complist = Get-Content "C:\computerList.txt"
## Iterate thru list##
foreach ($comp in $complist){
        ##Test Connection to machine##
$pingtest = Test-Connection -ComputerName $comp -Quiet -Count 1 -ErrorAction SilentlyContinue
        ##If machine pings search for file##
              if($pingtest){
invoke-command -computername $comp -scriptblock{get-package
"Java*" | uninstall-package -ErrorAction silentlycontinue}
}}
```

Installation

Using MSI Installers

For MSI packages, you can use msiexec:

$msiPath = "C:\Path\To\installer.msi"
Start-Process -FilePath "msiexec.exe" -ArgumentList "/i
$msiPath /quiet" -Wait

Using EXE Installers

Start-Process -FilePath "C:\Path\To\installer.exe" -
ArgumentList "/S" -Wait

A couple of notes here. The switches for silent installation and no user interaction are usually generic switches such as /quiet /S /n

TIP: You may find exact installation switches in PowerShell by going to the directory with the installer and calling the filename with the ? switch.

1. *installer.msi /?*
2. *.\installer.msi /?*
3. *installer.exe /?*
4. *.\installer.exe /?*

SYSTEM ADMINISTRATOR LEARNING POWERSHELL

NAKA MOTO

SYSTEM ADMINISTRATOR LEARNING POWERSHELL

NAKA MOTO

SYSTEM ADMINISTRATOR LEARNING POWERSHELL

NAKA MOTO

SYSTEM ADMINISTRATOR LEARNING POWERSHELL

NAKA MOTO